Time was, when the world went to the Vatican. Since the early days of Paul VI, the converse has been true, and John Paul II's overriding mission has been to take the Catholic Church and her teachings far and wide beyond the bounds of the Vatican City. This, his second pastoral visit to the United States, was, incredibly, his thirty-sixth foray among his vast, international flock.

Preparations for this city-hopping tour of the South and West were attended by continual and strident alarms for the Pope's safety. In the event, those of evil intent stayed away and allowed those for whom this papal progress might afford the experience of a lifetime to savor the moment. Protest proved another, and more real, matter. Jews complaining of the Pope's meeting, three months earlier, with Kurt Waldheim, canceled their invitation to meet John Paul, and only reinstated it ten days before it was due. Practising homosexuals were bitter about their exclusion from the Sacraments. Feminists bemoaned their outsider status. Abortionists protested against what they saw as unworkable theological theories. Large numbers of ordinary, mature, sophisticated Catholics grumbled audibly about the appointment of conservative bishops. And Fundamentalists protested at the visit, period.

That the Pope is nothing if not single-minded was amply demonstrated during this spectacular and vibrant tour. Clearly, he saw his job here as many-sided. He confirmed his support for his own bishops by insisting to all and sundry that dissent was "a grave error" and therefore intolerable. He avoided the risk (seen by some as imminent) of a conservative-liberal split in the American Church by concentrating his energies on the palpably less fortunate – Hispanics, farmworkers, AIDS sufferers, immigrants, oppressed ethnic minorities, Indians and blacks above all. In the face of their continuing problems, gripes over theological doctrine seemed bourgeois and eminently postponable.

In such circumstances, it may seem ironic that he could not work the miracle of pleasing all of the people all of the time. But to expect that is to misunderstand his mission. His call is fundamentally an invitation to repentance, not a condoning of what exists. A priest content to tell people what they want to hear is, in the eyes of God, nothing better than a false prophet. So he confined his teachings and pleadings to the very stuff of Roman Catholic dogma – the shunning of consumerism, the maintenance of human dignity from the womb to the deathbed, the abhorrence of violence, the sanctity of marriage, doctrinal infallibility and devotion to Mary.

As he landed, that first afternoon, in Miami, one television commentator unexpectedly enthused: "I guess you might say he represents just the best in us all – our yearning for the goodness that is buried in us." And, shortly before he left the States, an AIDS victim, his last months graced by John Paul's brief embrace, affirmed that "he has changed my life." There, bereft of controversy and protest, lies the essence of this latest pastoral progress.

Left: Pope John Paul II at prayer during his very first pastoral visit abroad – in Mexico in 1979.

Previous pages: 1987; welcoming crowds in Detroit.

A tumultuous welcome for the Pope on his visit to Mexico in 1979. Even a dawn earthquake failed to deter crowds from swarming into the center of Mexico City to hail the Holy Father at the start of a distinctive, colorful and historic tour. The early form of "Popemobile" (facing page) made him eminently visible yet, as always, frighteningly vulnerable, as the bevy of bodyguards reminds us. Between those spectacular public parades, the Pope was always at work: (top picture) consulting with a member of his staff during an inter city aircraft hop.

During a hectic and wide-ranging tour of Poland in 1979, John Paul met huge crowds in Warsaw, drew children towards him at Czestochowa, and celebrated Mass at the Jasna Gora shrine, where he met former concentration camp inmates.

11

"It is necessary to think with fear of how far hatred can go, how far man's destruction of man can go, how far cruelty can go." Accompanied by former prisoners (facing page inset), John Paul became the first Pope to visit Auschwitz (this page), where he saw the cell of the beatified priest Maximilian Kolbe, who sacrificed his own life to save a fellow prisoner. In a simple, touching gesture (above), the Holy Father remembered before God the four million souls who were wrenched from their homes and places of work to meet an inexorable fate in Nazi gas chambers. He also conducted an open-air Mass (left and far left) amid the barbed wire fences, prison blocks and watch-towers of what he termed "a place built on hatred and contempt for man." The event contrasted starkly with the more formal circumstances of the Mass at the Tomb of the Unknown Soldier in Warsaw's Victory Square (facing page) earlier in the tour.

Dublin's Phoenix Park became the focal point for hundreds of thousands of Irish men and women who witnessed the Pope celebrate the Eucharist among them. Perhaps this once-troubled land had never before known such an air of festivity, though it did not deflect the Holy Father from his central theme – a call for an end t the violence which continued to dog the people of Eire's neighbor, Ulster.

The Pope's memorable first visit to the United States of America began in Boston, but it was New York which provided the most spectacular welcome at the Yankee Stadium (facing page), and in the confetti-littered streets (top). The grueling tour, directly following that of Ireland, took His Holiness by way of Philadelphia and the Midwest, to Des Moines – where he celebrated Mass (top and overleaf) in a 600-acre expanse of farmland – to Chicago (left), and ultimately to the nation's capital (above).

18

John Paul II in America's most famous cities: celebrating Mass in New York (this page, and facing page, bottom right); and in Washington, D.C., where the Smithsonian buildings and the Capitol provided the setting for the concluding religious ceremonial of the tour.

Previous pages: with 60,000 soaked but loyal followers at Shea Stadium, New York. These pages: serenity and strain, confidence and concern, humor and pensiveness all captured by the camera during the Pope's U.S. tour.

The Pope greeting crowds during his first day in Lagos, in 1982, heralding a busy five-day tour of Nigeria's vibrant, teeming communities. Five major towns were visited and five Masses celebrated in public. "I would ask you," John Paul told his hosts, "to consider me one of your own, for indeed I come to this land as a friend and a brother to all its inhabitants."

A typical gesture, and one which is most closely associated with John Paul II – the kissing of the ground of each host country. Whether soil, turf or tarmac, the Pope has always made this symbolic embrace his first act on arrival, as at Honiara, capital of the Solomon Islands (right) in 1984. Below: crowds peep in wonder through security guards, photographers and prelates at their distinguished patriarchal visitor.

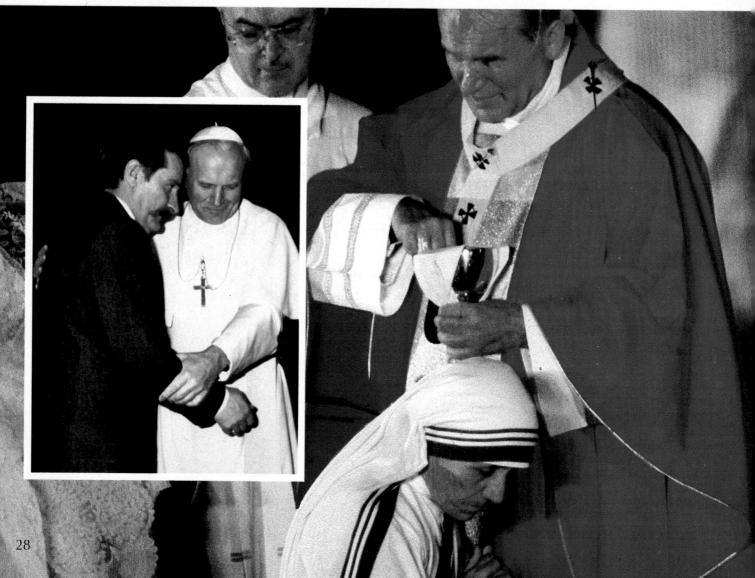

The many roles of a Pontiff. Facing page: hailed by admirers in Zaire in 1980 (top); with Lech Walesa during the Solidarity campaign (inset); and administering Holy Communion to Mother Teresa (bottom). This page: comforting a young girl in Bahia (top); passing jubilant Brazilian youngsters (above); acknowledging a Filipino welcome in 1984.

Previous pages: (left) a carpet of flowers for the Pope in Lisbon, Portugal, in 1982 and (right) a walk through Wembley Stadium in London to celebrate Mass. Facing page: with the King and Queen of Spain in 1982. This page: in the same year the Pope visited Argentina (top) in the wake of the Falklands conflict; the next year saw him in the midst of political upheaval in Nicaragua (above and right).

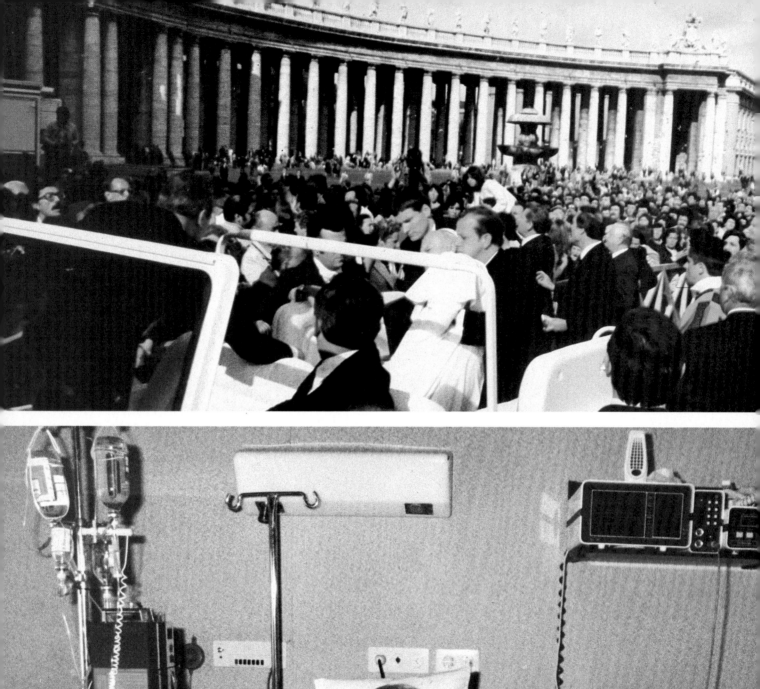

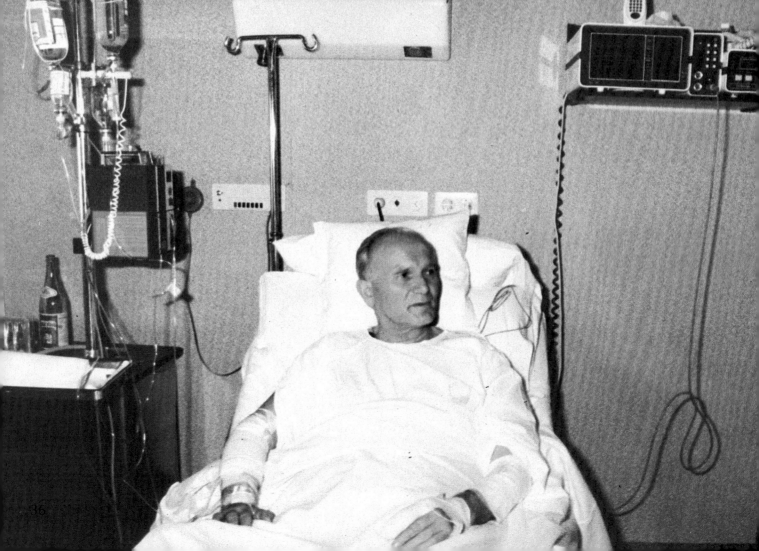

revious pages: John Paul's pilgrimage of faith to he Shrine of Our Lady of Lourdes in 1983. These ages: hatred turned to friendship; the dramatic noment of the attempt to assassinate the Pope acing page top) in May 1981; His Holiness' covery (facing page bottom) at the Gemelli ospital; and the eventual meeting and conciliation with his assailant, Mehmet Ali gca, at Rebibbia prison.

37

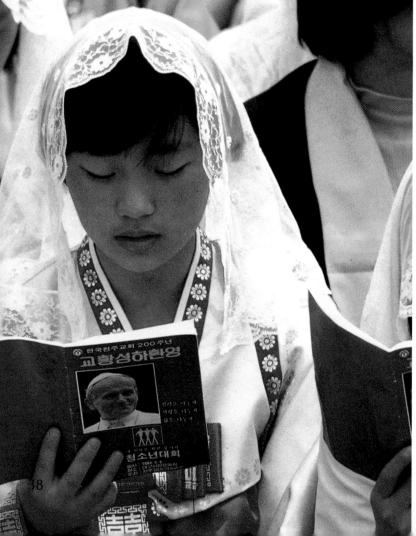

Pope John Paul's visit to South Korea in 1984 enveloped him in a riot of color. The brilliance of national dress complemented the dazzling effects of acres of flowers, brightly colored stands, and the massive white symbols of the Christian faith rising up into perfect blue skies. Here were huge, vibrantly attired choirs, audiences of the faithful, endless rows of adoring schoolchildren who shouted for him, waved flags and favors at him, or joined him in devotional worship. It was an overwhelming and emphatically hospitable beginning to a nine-day tour of the Far East that would also take the Pope to Papua New Guinea, the Solomon Islands and Thailand.

39

The Pope in Thailand (above) during a visit to the Royal Palace in Bangkok. Facing page: the Pope leaves after a visit to one of the city's sumptuous Roman Catholic temples. Top picture: an unusual location for John Paul as he combined his love of sport with his sense of communion with Nature in the Swiss Alps in 1984. Right: in prayerful concentration at Fribourg, Switzerland, that year.

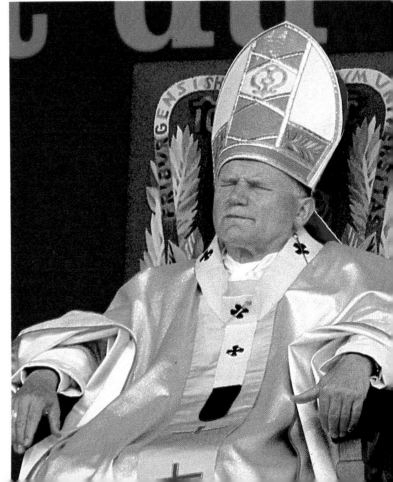

Previous pages: with President Reagan (left) in Alaska, and at Montreal, Canada. The Pope's Canadian tour was one of his most varied: (left) by the sea at St. John's; (below left) on the Rideau Canal in Quebec; (below) on a windswept open air site; (bottom, and overleaf left) at St. Anne de Beaupré; (facing page, and overleaf, right) attending Mass at Winnipeg.

44

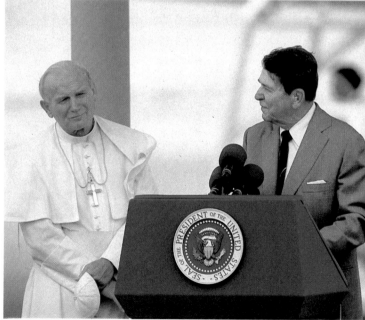

Shepherd I was the name of the aircraft which brought John Paul II to Miami to begin his second visit to the United States as Pope. There to greet him in brilliant sunshine were huge crowds (facing page, bottom), a bevy of cardinals (top) and – because the Pope is a Head of State – the Reagans (overleaf). Above and facing page, top: the Holy Father listening to a speech of welcome given by the President, who had flown down from Washington to make this one and only official contact of the entire ten-day tour.

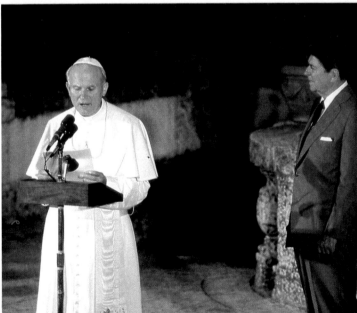

After the noise and excitement of his first welcome, the Pope spent a short time discussing world issues with President Reagan at Vizcaya, and made reply to his host's words of welcome (left, above and overleaf). The two men then took a short walk in the residence's beautiful formal garden (facing page). The following day, the Pope undertook his controversial meeting with Jewish leaders, to whom he vigorously defended his earlier meeting with Dr. Waldheim, and his predecessors' record of relationships with the wartime Axis powers.

Almost as if in direct defiance of the overwhelming numbers of non-Catholics in America's traditional Bible-belt – only two percent of Columbia's population is Catholic, compared with the southern state average of 5 percent – Pope John Paul paid a brief visit to this strongly evangelical South Carolina city (facing page, top). Despite some harsh words from Fundamentalists before his arrival, the day passed smoothly, and the Pope's meeting with Protestant churchmen was nothing if not friendly. He officiated at an inter-denominational Mass before flying to New Orleans.

The Crescent City welcomed the Pope with typical zest. The Olympia brass band played *When the Saints Go Marching In* as he left his aircraft, monks and nuns rushed to take their places in the crowds (facing page, bottom), and the streets were lined with the yellow and white flags as the papal motorcade, with the famous Popemobile at its center, made its way from the airport (this page). Overleaf: massive support from young and old as the Pope delivered one of several addresses in support of black rights to "an equal opportunity for a quality education and gainful employment."

gate E
girod stre
UNITY IN THE WORK OF SERVICE
SHARE
M
CELEBRATE
DREAM

Previous pages: (left) the Pope concelebrating Mass at the Superdome in New Orleans, and (right) officiating at St. Louis Cathedral on the first day of his visit. In contrast to the solemnity of that religious occasion (above), brass bands, security men and street artists were all in evidence in their own, perhaps more workaday, ways.

With the visit to New Orleans, the tour which many had feared would prove controversial seemed to have found a secure base. The Pope's Superdome call to black leaders to ensure "that all your black brothers and sisters may hear and embrace the saving and uplifting gospel... and must offer their own special solidarity of Christian love to all people who bear the heavy burden of oppression, whatever its physical or moral nature," seemed to reassure those who hoped he would not be deflected from his traditional teachings by the threat of hostility. Texas is one of the five main areas – Louisiana, Detroit, Washington, D.C. and New York City are the others – where America's black Catholics are rapidly increasing in number, so a visit to San Antonio afforded an appropriate opportunity to identify with them. These pages and overleaf: scenes from the spectacular outdoor Mass where 120,000 people heard the Pope speak partly in English, partly in Spanish.

The Pope next stopped – midway through his tour – at Phoenix, Arizona. At a ceremony attended by some 10,000 Indians, he spoke out against the "mistakes and wrongs" which American Indians had endured for centuries, and admitted that much of this had been suffered at the hands of religious devouts. "Unfortunately," he complained, "not all members of the Church have lived up to their responsibilities." A white eagle's feather, presented to him as a token of peace (above), seemed an apt sign of forgiveness.

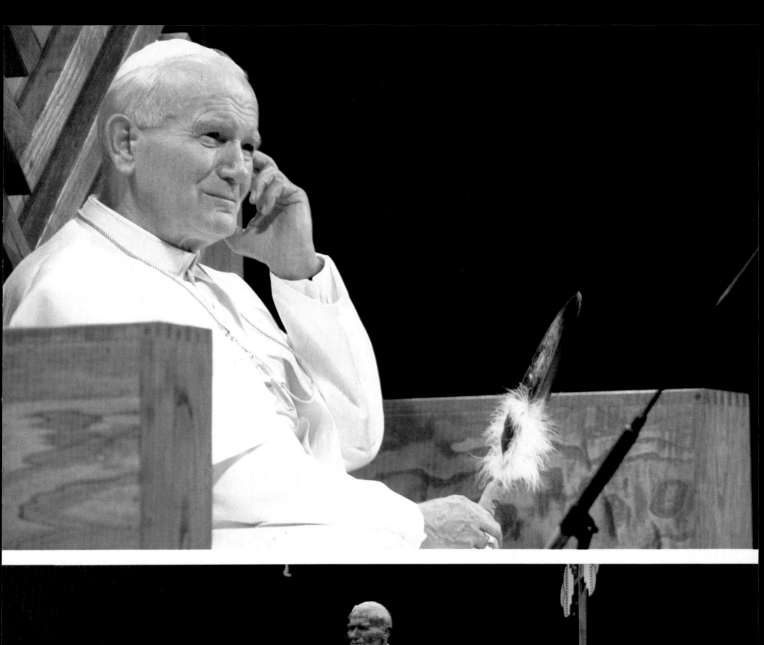

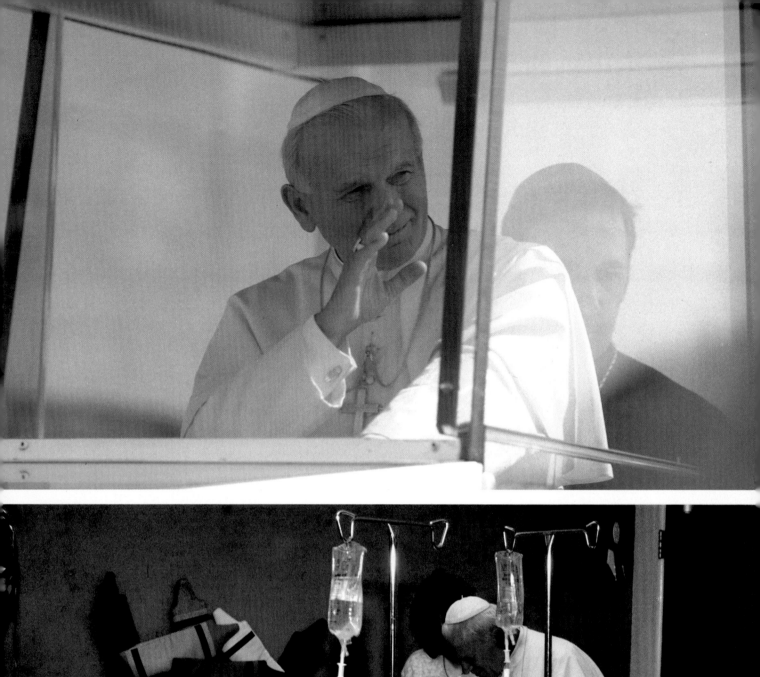

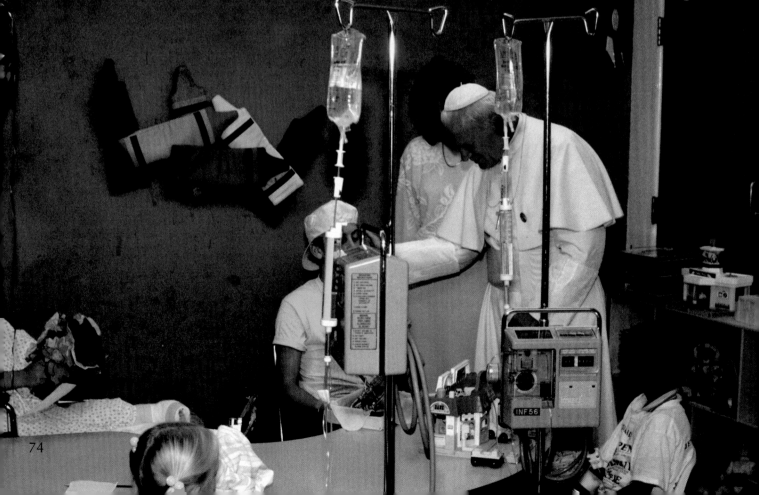

Previous pages and these pages: though the Indian contact proved the most colorful feature of the Phoenix visit, the Pope was on home ground working the crowds, meeting the young and sick, and moving among his people from the security of his ubiquitous Popemobile.

Top: The Pope being driven through the boulevards of Los Angeles. He met Mrs. Reagan again during a brief visit to a school (facing page), where he invited questions from the children. In reply to one about his safety, he said (left), "I am among children – no danger." Above: meeting, and (overleaf) addressing bishops at the San Fernando Mission.

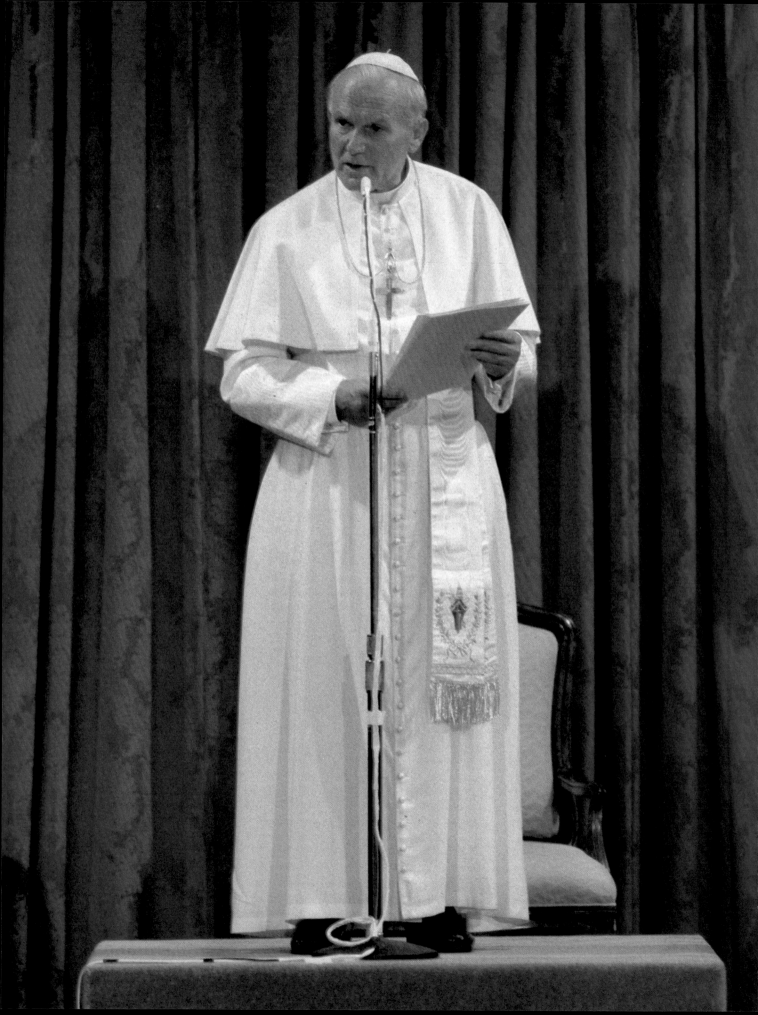

Previous page: crowds awaiting the Pope at Los Angeles' Coliseum (top); and welcoming him in Hollywood (bottom). These pages: symbolism (above) and the sheer love of theater (top) in evidence during the Pope's visit to Hollywood; while in downtown Los Angeles, a striking contrast is shown between modernity (left) and the fading glories of St. Vibiana's Cathedral (right).

During a short stopover at Monterey, the Pope met local mayors, including Clint Eastwood (above), after his arrival at the airport (facing page). He also visited Carmel Mission, one of the oldest in California, and held an open-air Mass at Laguna Seca (top), where he backed the cause of farmworkers against profiteering landowners and growers.

85

No visitor to San Francisco can prove the fact better than by a photograph of himself at the Golden Gate Bridge – and Pope John Paul II became the latest in a long line of distinguished sightseers (top). But there were more serious matters to attend to in this city of extremes, and the continuing AIDS crisis was one of them. Despite the taunts of the gay community, and the claims of their priesthood, the Pope insisted on being identified with those who had succumbed to the disease. "God loves you all, without limit, without distinction," he said during a visit to the Mission Dolores, where he met seventy AIDS victims. Among them was Brendan O'Rourke (left), a four-year-old who had been infected by icontaminated blood during a transfusion. Facing page and overleaf: the spectacular scenes at Candlestick Park, where the Pope held an open-air Mass.

No less than seventy percent of Detroit's population is Catholic, and nowhere are Detroit's Catholics more Polish than in the suburb of Hamtranck. So it made good sense for the Pope to pay his respects there (this page), a gesture well rewarded by a sunny reception in the midst of unseasonally drab weather. Facing page: the Pope celebrating Mass indoors and outdoors in Detroit.

91

The Pope's visit to Detroit was his third, though in truth the other two were made as Cardinal, not as Pontiff. Fellow Poles cheered him wildly on his arrival (right and facing page, top), and his recalling of the days of Solidarity in Poland – "its spirit rolls like a tidal wave over the face of the world," he said – renewed local affections for the man the people of Detroit claim as their own. For those who had committed their lives to the service of Christ, the briefest of meetings (below) was the moment of a lifetime.

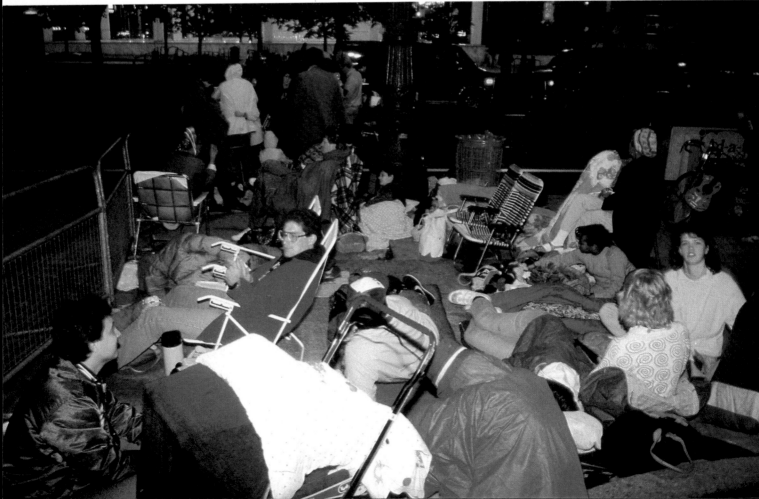

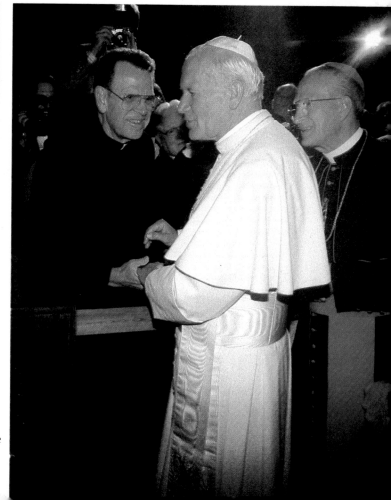

espite worsening weather, thousands of ordinary people waited
ours to be closest to him on his itinerary in Detroit (left). The
ghlight of the visit was the open-air Mass at the Pontiac
lverdome (top), attended by Vice-President George Bush, at which
retha Franklin sang (facing page, top) – one of the final events before
e Pope left to visit Fort Simpson, Canada.